W9-CHR-141

COPING WITH
BODY SHAMING

Natalie Chomet

Published in 2018 by The Rosen Publishing Group, Inc.
29 East 21st Street, New York, NY 10010

Copyright © 2018 by The Rosen Publishing Group, Inc.

First Edition

All rights reserved. No part of this book may be reproduced in any form without permission in writing from the publisher, except by a reviewer.

Library of Congress Cataloging-in-Publication Data

Names: Chomet, Natalie, author.
Title: Coping with body shaming / Natalie Chomet.
Description: New York, NY : Rosen Publishing, 2018. | Series: Coping |
Includes bibliographical references and index. | Audience: Grades 7-12.
Identifiers: LCCN 2017014238 | ISBN 9781508176879 (library bound) | ISBN 9781508178491 (paperback)
Subjects: LCSH: Body image—Juvenile literature. | Shame—Juvenile
literature. | Criticism, Personal—Juvenile literature. | Courtesy—Juvenile literature.
Classification: LCC BF697.5.B63 C46 2018 | DDC 306.4/613—dc23
LC record available at https://lccn.loc.gov/2017014238

Manufactured in China

CONTENTS

INTRODUCTION

I t's the 2017 Super Bowl halftime show, and Lady Gaga enters onto the field from above, suspended from a line. Her performance was a spectacle, as any halftime show should be, and it involved several costume changes, one of which included a crop top that exposed her midriff. Though her performance was a feat that showcased both her aerobic and vocal abilities, many of those who responded focused on one thing: her bare stomach. Body shamers took to the internet and commented on her belly via Twitter and Facebook, with comments that disparaged her for showing her stomach when it wasn't presentable enough by their standards. Conversely, many fans lashed out in response, commenting that her choice to show her less-than-perfect body was inspirational to them. Lady Gaga herself responded on Instagram with the comment, "I heard my body is a topic of conversation so I wanted to say, I'm proud of my body and you should be proud of yours too." The bottom line is that despite all the other aspects of her performance viewers could have focused on, her stomach became the focus because—though practically flat—it was still bigger than what we are accustomed to seeing in popular culture.

Many responses to Lady Gaga's performance at the 2017 Super Bowl halftime show were focused on what her body looked like rather than the act as a whole.

Body shaming is all around us; it comes from many directions and may take many forms. Superstar, supermodel, or super-normal, no one is exempt. No matter who you are or what you look like, chances are there have been times when you have been made to feel that your body is not normal, acceptable, or good enough. According to Harriet Brown's book, *Body of Truth,* in the first six months of 2014, a Google search for the word "obesity" resulted in twenty-seven million hits. The same Google search performed in February of 2017 comes up with eighty-seven million. Though not a scientific standard by any means, this shows our society's growing preoccupation with weight.

To be clear, shame over one's body is not confined to weight alone by any means, though it is a common focus for both men and women alike. Women and men of different races, sexual preferences, and cultures all navigate a complex and varied set of expectations regarding their appearance. Body shame, defined simply, is the result of someone making a person feel his or her body is not "correct" based on whatever standards of beauty the shamer may hold. Though anyone can be the target of body shaming, teens are in a unique position in this regard. As a teenager, you go through various stages of development. Puberty changes the body in gradual and dramatic ways, and it is hard enough to adjust to it on your own without the scrutiny of anyone else. The fact that each person's body goes through these changes at different paces and in different ways makes for more opportunities to compare and pass judgment. Who is growing a beard or needs a bra at the "right time," and who is supposedly late to the game? Social media only adds to this pressure and anxiety. The constant loop of sharing selfies and getting comments—both validating and disparaging—all based on your appearance makes it hard not to focus and pass judgment on your looks. So, how can you deal with it?

CHAPTER ONE

What a Shame

What do you see when you look in the mirror? Note if you automatically focus on things that you view as flaws and what they are. Body shaming can focus on the obvious and most prevalent things, such as weight or perceived fat, or small things, such as if your thighs touch when you stand straight, how tall you are, or if you have visible six-pack abs. The ideals of what is beautiful or handsome change based not just on gender but also on your cultural background.

Mirror, Mirror

In the United States, we tend to be concerned with slim bodies and bronzed, wrinkle-free skin. Around the world, other standards prevail: the Kayan tribe in Thailand consider women with long necks beautiful; the Karo tribe in Ethiopia

The women of Kayan Lahwi are known for wearing rings to elongate their necks in keeping with ancient tradition. Their long necks are a symbol of both beauty and status.

performs decorative scarring on women's bodies. A Photoshop experiment revealed that in Serbia, men with tattoos are considered attractive, while in South Africa, men with dark skin and defined abs are considered attractive. As a teen, there are so many phases that you go through physically, chances are you aren't 100 percent comfortable in your own skin without all the added outside pressure!

Seeking the "Perfect" Post-Baby Body

There's also the added pressure for women to get back into shape quickly after pregnancy. Many celebrities—including Kim Kardashian, Kate Hudson, and Kate Middleton, to name a few—have been shamed in the media for not having the "ideal" body after a pregnancy. Or on the flip side, a celebrity who gets her beach body back quickly after a pregnancy is praised in the media. This perpetuates an unhealthy and unrealistic expectation for new moms. Celebrities will have much more access to resources that will help them achieve this goal: nannies, personal trainers, dietitians, and more. Most people won't be able to spend six hours a day doing cardio and yoga routines to snap back into shape right after having a baby. And why should they even want to? It perpetuates both an unrealistic goal and an emphasis on appearance over well-being. A new mom should instead be focusing on letting her postpartum body recover, her health, and the health of a new baby.

Women in particular are subject to pressure to conform to many beauty ideals that seem nearly impossible to exist in one single body at once: small waist, large breasts (but not too large), a gap between skinny thighs, but also a curvy backside (but not too prominent). If women all believed they needed to have every one of these attributes, who wouldn't look in the mirror and find they came up short?

It isn't only girls and women who are often dissatisfied with their bodies. Boys and men feel the pressure, too. For both girls and guys, the overexposure to images of bodies considered to be ideal takes its toll on body image and self-esteem. Boys and men are increasingly unhappy with their own bodies for one reason or another (most often because of a perceived lack of muscularity). In 2012, 90 percent of teen boys exercised with the specific goal of bulking up, and all signs point to this trend increasing over time, according to an article for *Preservation* by Marla E. Eisenberg, Melanie Wall, and Diane Neumark-Sztainer.

Teens in particular are in a position to feel less than satisfied with how they look since they're still developing and getting used to their changing bodies themselves. And often, putting others down is an easy way to give yourself a quick boost of self-esteem. It's also a form of social bonding, but the quick surge is more of a Band-Aid on the problem than a solution. You won't feel great about yourself just by making others feel worse. And chances are, if the bonds of friendship you form with your social circle are mainly based on superficiality, they're going to prove awfully breakable in the end. So between cultural norms, the awkwardness of puberty, and social pressure, how can you combat them all and feel good in your own skin? The first step is identifying the sources of body shame.

The Normalization of Abnormal

The shame associated with not looking a certain way, the way that you "should," does not come out of nowhere. Our society shapes our expectations and opinions on what defines a beautiful or even just plain acceptable body. Media as well as the behavior of those around us start to shape these perceptions earlier than you might think. Many studies have shown that children as young as three or four years old are already afraid of getting fat. The possible sources of this fear are vast: whether it comes from their families at home, books, television, doctors, teachers, games, or other children, the message is coming through loud and clear. Even at such a young age, they already understand that there is a way you are not supposed to look.

It is problematic enough that we are processing this societal pressure to look thin when we are only toddlers. The images we are exposed to each day in the media make matters worse by perpetuating beauty

You may be surprised at how young we start absorbing and internalizing societal beauty standards from our environment and the people around us.

ideals that are often physically impossible. Imagine you are traveling to school in the morning. If you take public transit, you may find your eyes resting on an ad in your bus or train car. By car, you'll likely pass billboards that depict models posing in unnatural ways or celebrities whose features appear smooth and flawless. Stop at a deli or newsstand to get a pack of gum or a snack and you're confronted with countless magazine covers touting swimsuit-clad supermodels or boasting a new thirteen-day, fat-busting miracle diet.

Next time you see an image on an ad or magazine cover, ask yourself, what's wrong with this picture? Nearly all of the images that bombard our conscious and subconscious minds each day are altered to achieve the supposed perfection we find ourselves striving for in real life. Instead of doing this through diet and exercise or even surgery, these bodies are

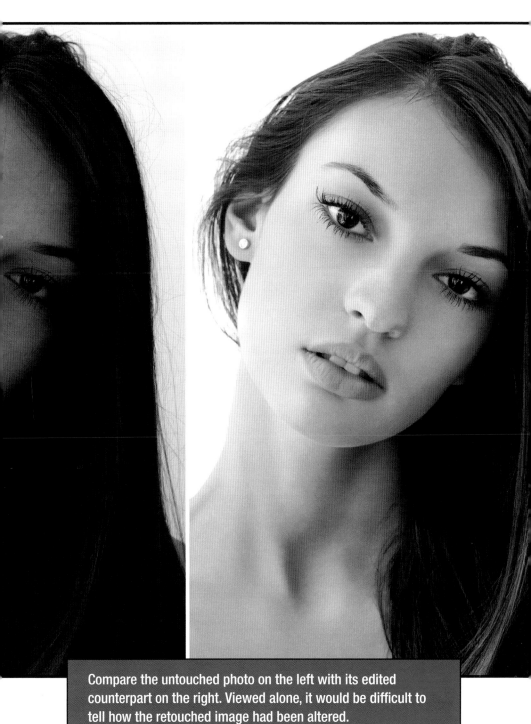

Compare the untouched photo on the left with its edited counterpart on the right. Viewed alone, it would be difficult to tell how the retouched image had been altered.

enhanced digitally. Many people are likely familiar with the concepts of airbrushing and Photoshopping images to make them look a certain way, but it is still surprising how much the images you see each day are perfected with the help of technology. No wonder our perceptions are so warped.

"The normalization of the abnormal" is a phrase that the Beauty Redefined website has coined to explain this phenomenon. The site—whose mission is to reinvent what beauty means and to reject and question harmful messages about body image—explains just why the practice of digital manipulation is dangerous to our self-image: "Digitally slimming women's bodies [...] and removing signs of life like pores, gray hairs, and wrinkles aren't just casual decisions based on aesthetic preferences of a few editors—they are profit-driven decisions to create false ideals for females to seek after in hopes of someday attaining. These hopes are largely driven by desire to be found attractive, loved, appear healthy, and ultimately, happy." Though the focus of this website is women's self-image, it's not just women who are victims of this practice. Whether it is a digitally imposed thigh gap on a woman or a man with an impossibly defined six-pack or poreless face, there's no doubt that technology has made our expectations impossible to attain.

Woman Versus Machine

Though it isn't a secret that actors' and models' images in magazines are often altered, the effect is starkly different from how they appear in reality, and it is one we have grown accustomed to seeing. Some celebrities, like Lena Dunham, are less than pleased with this phenomenon and have taken a public stance against it. The blog Jezebel obtained the untouched photos from a shoot the writer and actress of HBO's *Girls* did for *Vogue* and published the before and after, with arrows to draw attention to the details that were changed. These changes included making her waist smaller, erasing smile lines and shadows under the eyes, and covering up and altering her cleavage.

In contrast, the cover of the February 2017 issue of *Glamour* features Dunham in short shorts with her *Girls* costars, without any airbrushing done. She expressed happiness that her body was "on full imperfect display" on the cover of a magazine read by millions of women. Lena Dunham isn't the only one to publicly take a stand against Photoshopping and airbrushing. In 2015, Kate Winslet signed a contract with L'Oréal that bans retouching of her photos. This was in line with her criticism of *GQ* when they extensively altered a cover image of the actress in 2003.

Close to Home

Pressure to look a certain way doesn't only come from images in the media. Whether it's the aspects of your appearance your family praises the most or the way your mom talks about her own body, your own conceptions of what's beautiful and what's not start to form early and may come from your own home. Family dynamics can play a large part in how you see yourself.

Think of home in a broader sense. The overall culture of Western civilization today sees skinny as beautiful and muscular as handsome. But in other parts of the world, the standards of beauty are not the same. In Brazil, for example, a curvy, tanned woman is considered beautiful—perhaps too curvy or not slim enough by current American standards. In Japan, women with crooked teeth are considered cute and youthful. (You can even buy dentures to achieve the look!) Surgery bandages indicating a recent nose job are worn with pride by women in Iran, believe it or not.

The aesthetics of what looks good to us is more than a case of taste. It is often an indication of what current society values. A quick scan of America through time can show how these ideals change with what's going on in the world: in the 1910s, the

Marilyn Monroe's hourglass figure was the pinnacle of womanly beauty in the 1950s, which contrasts sharply with flat, androgynous shapes favored in the 1920s through 1960s.

androgynous, thin flapper was attractive during a time when women were fighting for the right to vote; in the 1950s, Marilyn Monroe's curvy figure that emphasized the feminine was the beauty ideal when Americans were experiencing post–World War II pressure to breed and grow the population and economy. When a country is going through a time of poverty or famine, plumpness can become not only an attractive look but a symbol of status as well.

There may be some evolutionary reasons why we gravitate toward people who look like us and, by extension, shun or ignore those who appear different in some way. We, as humans, are social creatures, and in early times, our survival depended on banding together for protection and strength. The ability to tell the difference between friend and foe was distilled to quick categorizations. We assessed the people around us to see if we were alike in obvious, fundamental ways and therefore "friend." These quick groupings of friends and enemies were often based on appearance. Today, our social identities are often shaped by what we have in common with the people around us. Though our survival no longer depends on it, we still try to conform to those around us to fit in socially. Some of those groupings may be based on religion, where you grew up, and common interests or hobbies. Many others may unconsciously still be based on appearance.

Have you ever noticed that the kids that sit alone at lunch are often the ones who are considered different in some way?

If we look at where our ideals of appearance come from, what they symbolize, and their impact on how we relate to each other, we can begin to recognize and unpack why we feel unhappy in our own skins.

CHAPTER TWO

The Many Faces of Shaming

Whether it was on purpose or done unconsciously, you can probably think of a time that you have been body shamed by a friend, family member, or someone on social media. Subtle microaggressions and blatant bullying can hurt in different ways, but whether it is someone close to you or a bully who criticizes your body, it never feels good. Examining the root of where the shaming comes from helps give you tools to navigate these situations.

The Student Body

There's a reason the schoolyard bully is a cliché: kids can be cruel, and everyone has experienced what it feels like to be on the tail end of a joke or insult at school or among peers. Going through

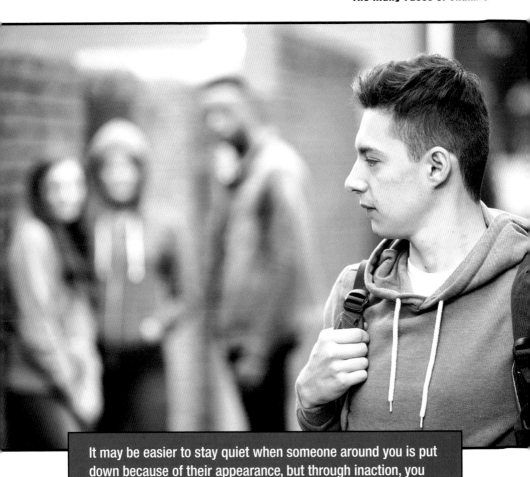

It may be easier to stay quiet when someone around you is put down because of their appearance, but through inaction, you allow the bullying to become the norm.

adolescence comes with a unique set of pressures. Though there are the obvious ones that come from your family and your school to do well and be successful, there are also the many pressures of finding a niche or group of friends where you are liked and accepted. For most, this translates to fitting in or simply trying not to stand out too much. The way family and society shapes us, by the time you reach your teen years you have a set idea of what normal means, and more often than not, it's easier and more appealing to blend in and conform to those standards than to break the ranks.

Fitting in may sound easy enough, but a problem arises when someone's body does not conform with what peers consider normal. You don't have to actively bully people for looking different to make them feel bad. Not standing up for them or deciding to take the easy route and not socialize with them just perpetuates the problem. Isabel Song, a contributor to Huffpost Teen, expressed frustration over how the shaming perpetuates itself: "Instead of joining together against these bodily insecurities, we go after each other like dogs. Guys refuse to consider girls who aren't skinny and sexy, and girls refuse to consider guys who don't have abs and muscles all over their bodies. Guys pick on other 'weaker' guys, and girls pick on 'ugly' girls. Why can't we just say no and refuse to buy into this ideal of what we're supposed to look like? Why can't we stop pulling each other down and stop tearing at each other's insecurities?"

It's easy to stand quietly by or make a comment or joke when someone is being shamed for looking different. The human brain doesn't fully form until we hit our twenties, and our identities and personalities are still shaping, too. Add a surge of hormones and you've got a volatile recipe for personal insecurities.

Being aware that everyone is worried about seeming cool and having friends can give some context to why body shaming happens—especially with other teens.

Attack of the Faceless Bullies

We live in a time when people regularly take to the internet as a way to freely share their opinions without fear of consequence, so it follows that body shaming often takes place virtually. The anonymity makes it easier to say whatever comes to mind, and the lack of face-to-face confrontation means that the shamers don't have to see or acknowledge the results of their words. Add to the mix a heaping dose of imagery of bodies displayed online—from selfies to dating profile pictures to celebrity photos—and you have plenty of openings for anyone to pick someone else's appearance apart.

To make matters worse, many body-related "challenges" quickly start trending online and encourage people to post pictures of parts of their body to see if they are acceptable or ideal according to unrealistic standards. Examples of this are: the iPhone 6 knees challenge where women place an iPhone 6 over their knees and if it covers them both, then they are the right size; the belly button challenge where the participant wraps an arm behind her back to see how close she can get her fingers around to her belly button (implying

Technology and social media allow competitions that concern body image to catch on quickly. It's easy to take a picture and post it for your followers to see and comment on.

that the closer it is, the thinner and fitter she is); and the collarbone challenge, in which women in China posted images of themselves with stacks of coins in their collarbone gap to show how pronounced it is. No matter how absurd or arbitrary these challenges seem, they keep catching on—yet another way to perpetuate unrealistic body ideals and compare people's bodies to each other's, not to mention the stream of comments on those bodies that each image gets.

The downside of our current culture being oversaturated with unrealistic body images and seemingly endless negative comments online is obvious. But its effect may be even more serious than we are aware of. A Yahoo health survey done in 2016 yielded the result that 94 percent of teenage girls in America have been body shamed online. Many of the behaviors that men and teenage boys display online, such as the images they choose for their profile pictures, show that the self-consciousness our selfie culture perpetuates doesn't only apply to women.

Is there an upshot to the digital discourse about our bodies that seems to never stop? Just as the belly button challenge can become a trend, so can body-positive narratives. People famous and unknown have posted video responses, images with captions, hashtags, and entire blogs devoted to combating body shaming and promoting body positivity. Whether a post addresses specific shamers and calls them out for adding their toxic voice to the world or simply shows someone who is comfortable in his or her own skin, these efforts have made body shaming a public conversation. For every voice that speaks up against body shaming online, there could be dozens of others who see that and take solace in the fact that the narrative is changing.

What's Love Got to Do with It?

Have you ever been in a relationship or had a crush on someone who caused you to feel that his or her affection depended on you looking a certain way? Whether it's how the person treated you or actual things he or she said, the feeling remained that you had to be skinny enough/muscled enough/tall enough (you get the idea) to be worthy of attention and love.

These toxic dynamics can occur subconsciously and unintentionally. The person you're dating could

Celeb Example

When actor Wentworth Miller found himself the subject of a meme because of his recent weight gain, he used it as a platform to open up a public conversation about suicide and depression. His open letter response explained the battle with suicidal thoughts and depression that caused him to put on weight: "Now, when I see that image of me in my red t-shirt, a rare smile on my face, I am reminded of my struggle. My endurance and my perseverance in the face of all kinds of demons. Some within. Some without." He ended his post with a list of links to helpful resources for people battling suicidal thoughts and depression.

In an interview, actress Emma Stone addressed being criticized online for being too skinny: "I've seen a lot of comments that say, 'Eat a sandwich' or 'She looks sick.' I've been looking at myself in the mirror being mean to myself. I'm not sick. I eat sandwiches ... We shame each other online. We're always too skinny or too fat or too tall or too short ... It bothers me because I care so much about young girls. We're shaming each other and we're shaming ourselves, and it sucks."

(continued on the next page)

(continued from the previous page)

Actress Emma Stone has expressed how hard it is for her to feel good about her own body when faced with constant scrutiny from being in the public eye.

These kinds of public responses to body shaming that celebrities have had show not only that you can stand up to bullies, but that everyone deals with personal struggles—famous or not—and you never know what a person has gone through or is going through based on appearance alone.

make you feel that you should be satisfied with whatever you get, whether it's cold detachment or emotional abuse, because he or she has made you believe that you cannot find anything better. It probably speaks more to that person's lack of self-confidence that he or she has to make you feel small and unworthy of affection, in order to have power.

Friends can do this just as easily as romantic partners can. Photographer Jade Beall, who takes unaltered photos of women as part of "A Beautiful Body Project," puts it this way: "Find a community that can see YOU. Don't hang out with people who are obsessing about how they need to be different to be happy ... I stopped hanging out with people who complain about themselves all the time, and it's a work in progress; a practice. But I want to be around those who work towards self-love instead of self-hatred. I have enough of that on my own."

This is a great and important concept, though it can be hard to achieve when you're going through a time in your life where your body, hormones, brain, and identity are still developing and changing. But these friendships, relationships, and communities do exist, and you can build them yourself. Notice what your friends or your date spend a lot of time talking about. Is it dieting or how this shirt makes his arms look? Or is it the last episode of the show you both like to watch or that awesome concert coming up?

Perhaps you aren't in a relationship, but you feel that you can't meet someone who will want to date you until you make your body look a certain way, whether that means bulking up, losing a few pounds, or wearing the right kind of makeup or clothes. Though advertisements may lead us to believe that only certain body types are attractive or worthy of romantic attention, this is not the case in reality. No one, including yourself, should make you feel that your body is not good enough. The myth that fat people, short people, or skinny people can and should only date their own kind is just that: a myth! People with all sorts of body types are attracted to one another, and personalities that mesh come in all shapes and sizes. Next time you find yourself questioning this, look around you in reality (not just the movies or online) and you'll see it's true.

The Problem with Apples and Trees

The way you're raised can shape the way you see yourself and the world around you. If your parents perceive themselves in negative ways, it's easy for that practice to rub off on you and how you see yourself. Even casual comments or jokes about fat or unwanted body types can lead to a self-consciousness about your own body. Measuring yourself against siblings or other family members is another way you can start to feel insecure about your appearance. Perhaps other members of the family have a habit of comparing you against others: "She's the tall one," or "he's the athletic one."

Surprisingly, it's not just negative comments about your body that can trigger insecurities. Imagine if a grandparent, aunt, or uncle compliments the flatness of your stomach or how you've stretched out from a growth spurt. This can trigger an anxiety or pressure to maintain the attributes that your family praises as attractive. Comparing yourself to others can distort your own self-image. In Harriet Brown's book, a woman whose daughter was anorexic says that her own body image began to change as she accepted her daughter's sick, emaciated body as normal. "Other people's bodies began to look too large, oddly

Comparing yourself to family members is an easy trap to fall into, especially if you're a sibling. Others may compare you to a family member without realizing the dynamic it creates.

distorted—especially my own, which came to feel grotesque. [...] I tried consciously reminding myself over and over that my body hadn't changed size, and that the emaciation of anorexia was abnormal, not my own body." A far less extreme example of this is realizing you are on the shorter side of your high school class because within the confines of your own family, you're the tall one. How you measure up is always going to be relative to whom you see and spend the most time around, so comparing yourself to others won't ever give you an accurate sense of your own body.

Myths & FACTS

Myth: Skinny people never feel shame about their bodies.

Fact: No matter their weight, everyone experiences shame about their body at some time or another. Our world today may prize being thin, but thinness does not directly correlate to having high self-esteem or a positive body image.

Myth: Girls are more self-conscious about their bodies than boys.

Fact: Studies have shown that boys are more likely to see themselves as underweight or not muscular enough, while girls often obsess over thinness. The medical director of an eating disorders program at Children's Hospital Colorado said that 25 percent of her patients are boys. It goes to show that boys have anxiety about their bodies, too, and it may be more common than you think.

Myth: I will feel better about my body when it's thinner/curvier/more muscled [fill in the blank].

Fact: That's not usually the case. If you want to lose weight, you may go on a diet and achieve your goal, but you may end up fixating on your weight even more than before. If your mind is trained to focus on your body's flaws (whatever you think they are), that's all you will see. You have to be happy with yourself as you are, and seeing the "right" number on a scale doesn't equal loving your body.

CHAPTER THREE

Tools to Cope

After examining all the directions from which body shaming can come, the logical question is how to deal with those people, situations, and words that wound? Each situation will come with its own set of unique factors: the person doing the shaming, if it is overt or unintentional, and most importantly, how YOU feel. Perhaps a situation will arise that will give you the perfect platform to make people understand something they may not have known about you, the way Wentworth Miller did. Explaining how the words make you feel or something that is going on in your life may give someone who hurt you new insight into you and, along with it, compassion. It's also entirely possible that you may not feel comfortable with or safe enough for confrontation, especially when it comes to something as personal as comments about your body. There is not only one right way to deal with a situation, but there are tools that can help you cope with each one.

Wentworth Miller is a British-American actor, model, and screenwriter who used an online meme mocking his weight gain as a platform to speak out about his struggles with depression.

Confronting a Shamer

The idea of confronting someone who has just said something to hurt you can be daunting. But this doesn't mean you're picking a fight. There are several ways you can approach someone who has body shamed you, and most aim to diffuse the situation. The simplest and most straightforward approach is explaining why a comment is hurtful. If a friend tells you the dress you tried on isn't flattering on your body type or if someone says your crush won't like you because you're not his or her type, calmly break down, in straightforward terms, why these words hurt you.

If you feel safe enough to do so, you can use the situation as a teachable moment. It could be an opportunity to explain what body positivity is, why it is important to you, and how you practice it in your life. It's easy to slip into the habit of criticizing your own body and those around you or focusing on the flaws

Explaining why comments someone made were hurtful to you can be a direct, effective way to keep them from making you or someone else feel shamed in the future.

as you have been trained to view them. If you feel comfortable enough to break this down for the person, then there's a good chance he or she could benefit from a dose of body positivity, too.

Here's a tactic that is a little counterintuitive and may be difficult to do: sympathize. Can you contextualize this person for yourself and understand where some of the hurtful comments stem from? Take the kid who just called you "chicken legs" in the locker room. What's his story? It's possible he could be having a bad day; it's even more likely that he doesn't have a high level of body confidence or self-esteem in general. There are many reasons why people put others down, but more often than not, it has to do with something they are going through and less to do with you. This may be difficult because who wants to sympathize with someone who has just hurt and humiliated you? But if you can do it, in the end, you'll come away with more awareness, poise, and compassion, and less of the hurt than before. Putting yourself in the other person's shoes may help take a little bit of the sting out of his or her actions.

The simplest tactic and often the wisest one is to disengage. Just like it's often wiser to walk away from a fight than to be on the offensive, sometimes it's better to make the active choice not to respond and therefore end the interaction. People who are body shaming you are looking for a response to show that what they have done has hurt you. If you don't give them anything back, they will run out of steam and you can walk away with your head held high. This choice will likely be the best option for dealing with those shamers who are combative or those who you know aren't worth the trouble. If this isn't someone you have a close relationship with, you won't lose much if you cut ties.

This tactic may also come into play when it comes to interactions with friends, family, and significant others. You have the right to decide that you don't want to go into a detailed explanation of why they hurt you or to have a tiring fight about it. If the person who has body shamed you is someone you want to stay close with, eventually you will have to confront him or her and try to repair the damage to your relationship, but that doesn't mean you have to do it as soon as the shaming occurs. Take the time you need to approach the situation with a level head.

The bottom line is that no matter which strategy you employ to confront a body shamer, you must also remember to be kind to yourself. Body shaming hurts, and having an emotional response is normal. The best way to get over the pain of this is to let yourself experience the emotions that body shaming brings to the surface so that you can move through them and ultimately move on.

To Respond or Retreat

A friend using body-negative language: Be honest with your friend that his or her body-negative talk (even if it's referring to him- or herself) is making you uncomfortable and explain why it does.

A repeat offender: If the hurtful talk keeps coming up with the same friend, despite your efforts and explanation, you may want to consider if the positives of this relationship outweigh the negatives. If not, you may be better off parting ways.

A possibly serious problem: If you or a friend is showing signs of an eating disorder, it's time to turn to outside help. Take note if body shaming has caused you or a friend to change eating habits or gain or lose weight. These could be signs of a possible eating disorder as well. Go to a trusted adult, such as a parent or school counselor as soon as possible. Eating disorders are diseases that can cause serious harm, so make sure you or the person you know gets help. You can also call the National Eating Disorders Association (NEDA) at 800-931-2237 or text "NEDA" to 741741 to be connected with a trained volunteer.

Where Did That Come From?

Sometimes body shaming isn't about the body being shamed at all. In order to break down negative comments about your body or someone else's, it helps to look deeper than the surface of the negative remark to what's at its root. It could be the low self-esteem of the person doing the shaming that's driving the negativity: putting you down to boost his or her own confidence, quieting insecurities, or even redirecting negative attention that could otherwise have been focused on him or her.

There are times when people use negative talk about someone's body as an easy excuse to voice criticisms about the person's character. You may notice this with figures who are in the public eye. Chris Christie has gotten many fat-shaming comments from the media, colleagues, and bystanders over the course of his career as governor of New Jersey. If you pay attention to the content of the remarks or the people they come from, you may start to see a trend. It's easy to take a cheap shot at someone's weight or physical appearance, but is that the real problem that most shamers have with Christie, or do they disagree with his policies? Better to voice your opinion about his stance on issues, his trustworthiness as a politician, or the actions he has taken than to make comments about his body. If you notice this type of remark come

Chris Christie is an American politician, lobbyist, and attorney. He was the fifty-fifth Governor of New Jersey, serving two terms from January 2010 to January 2018.

up in conversation with someone you know, you can cut through the superficial by questioning the criticism: "What does weight/appearance have to do with what kind of person he is?" Even if a comment like that seems too direct, you can still steer the conversation to the actions or opinions that the person might take issue with rather than appearance-based remarks.

We know we will always have moments where we encounter negative body commentary, but knowing how to handle it when this kind of talk comes up is half the battle. Depending on the context and your comfort level, you can be up front about how that talk makes you feel; shift the conversation so that any remarks are focused on the actions or character of someone rather than his or her body, or give the shamer context to take away the power of his or her words.

Combat Cruelty with Compassion

If someone is purposely saying hurtful things about your body, chances are the person wants a reaction. Whether it's to make you feel less worthy and humiliated or to get a cheap laugh from others, he or she is seeking a response. Instead of seeing a bully, if you can look at that person and see the insecurities that motivate the behavior, the shameful remarks might not pack the punch that they once did. Try to avoid fighting cruelty with more cruelty because no matter what your body looks like, no body type is free from issues of insecurity. Everyone has experienced shame at some time in their lives, skinny or not. All bodies are worthy of respect and kindness, and sinking to the level of someone who has body shamed you will just perpetuate the problem.

Besides the effect that body shaming may have on the person doing the shaming, it will likely take its toll on you, too. The shamer may experience (or hope to experience) a brief boost in self-confidence in putting you down. The other effect his or her comments may have is to amplify or give voice to self-criticism in you that you might not have even been aware of before. "Do my legs look too skinny in these shorts?" "Are my shoulders really that broad?" It's possible that inner dialogue has been taking place all along, but having someone point out a perceived flaw will only make that voice stronger.

No matter what you look like, you have likely experienced shame about your body at some point in your life. Remember that the same is true for the people around you.

A good start to preventing those negative thoughts from taking over is to take note of when you hear them creeping in. Try to stop yourself from passing judgment on your own body, whether it takes the form of a critical thought or a half-joking, self-deprecating remark. You may not be able to control the people around you, but you are in control of the things you tell yourself. When you become more aware of that inner voice, you will be able to gain more control over how you think about yourself, too.

CHAPTER FOUR

Did I Shame Someone?

"**O**h God, I can't wear that today, I feel too bloated." Body shame takes many forms and can spread in quiet, subtle ways. When you make a joke about yourself or comment on how

Trying on clothes that don't fit can be demoralizing. Try not to be critical of yourself, though. It will only make you feel worse.

much you ate, you may not realize you are body shaming yourself. Even if you do, did you ever stop to think about how those comments make the people around you feel?

It's Not Just About You

Maybe you've made a comment about the "burrito baby" in your stomach after a lunch out to your favorite Mexican restaurant, said that you can't pull off a certain type of clothing because it's not flattering for your body type, or told someone you were going on a diet/exercise regime to get a beach body or undo the damage from the holidays. At least one of these scenarios will likely seem familiar. If you've ever engaged in a conversation similar to this one, you may be able to detect why it's

Your fashion choices should be based on what makes you feel good about yourself—not what others deem acceptable or flattering.

detrimental to your own self-image, but what you may not be aware of is its effect on those around you.

When you put yourself down for a physical attribute that you see as a flaw, whether it's your weight, muscle mass, or body shape, you're communicating more than self-criticism. If you say to a friend, for example, "I feel fat," you're telling that friend a few things between the lines, one being that you think that it's bad to be fat. Though we are all most critical of ourselves, our talk about ourselves can be interpreted as how we see the people around us, as well. Your comment may cause your friend, who may be bigger than you, to compare herself to you and end up feeling worse. "If she thinks she's fat, then I must be huge!" No matter how they look, if you body shame yourself, you're going to cause the people around you to shift their focus to their own bodies and find flaws just like you did. Your own insecurity can validate the insecurities of those around you. If you tell your friends that you're not muscular enough, they'll see that as something you value, and if they aren't muscular either, their bodies won't be accepted as attractive or good enough either.

Cut the Clothing Commentary

Even if you aren't saying something openly about someone else's body, you can still be implicitly commenting on it. For example, if you've commented that a certain item of clothing isn't flattering on you or on a friend's body, it may sound like you're talking about the item of clothing, but you're really talking about the person's body. If saying that clothing isn't right for the person wearing it sounds like a criticism of the clothing to you, think again. Taking the logic of that statement a bit further means that certain bodies are not supposed to wear this type of clothing while it's perfectly acceptable for other types of bodies to wear them. Putting it in these terms reveals how discriminatory and hurtful that can feel to the wearer.

People say things like this all the time, and the effect is that we have set ideas as a society of what is acceptable and is not acceptable for people of different sizes to wear. This issue comes up not only on an interpersonal level but on a commercial one as well. There have been several examples of body shaming by clothing companies, many with disastrous results. The female athletic wear company Lululemon had such a case, which came up in a 2013 interview on Bloomberg News. When Lululemon's founder and chief executive officer Chip Wilson was asked about the recall of some excessively thin (and as a result overly sheer and quick to pill) black yoga pants, he made it sound like the issue wasn't with the way the clothing was made but with the bodies wearing them: "They don't work for certain women's bodies. Because even our small sizes would fit an extra-large. It's more about the rubbing through

Lululemon's chief executive officer Chip Wilson blamed women's bodies instead of admitting that a line of recalled yoga pants were poorly manufactured. He stepped down that same year.

the thighs and how much you're using it." These comments caused a public outcry, understandably, because the CEO ostensibly blamed women's bodies for the manufacturing defect of the yoga pants. Though he created an apology video, most weren't satisfied. That same year, Wilson stepped down as chairman because of the controversy his comments created.

Another company that ran into trouble with body-related discrimination is Abercrombie & Fitch. Also in 2013, CEO Mike Jeffries was called to task regarding some comments he made on A&F's marketing strategy that had come to light: "Candidly, we go after the cool kids. We go after the attractive all-American kid with a great attitude and a lot of friends. A lot of people don't belong [in our clothes], and they can't belong. Are we exclusionary? Absolutely." This statement could have sparked outrage all on its own, but coupled with the company's refusal to offer women's clothing in size extra large (although it existed on the men's

The outfit you put on should make you feel good about yourself. No colors, patterns, or styles should be off limits for you because of your body type.

side), it earned Abercrombie & Fitch heavy criticism in the media. It was clear that this exclusionary marketing strategy hurt the company's business, though it did spur multiple body-positive social media campaigns launched in response. After a year, though the media attention had lessened, the story was still being covered. The brand closed stores, and its stock dropped lower than it had been in years.

Even though overtly saying that certain bodies are not meant to wear a type of clothing is unacceptable in the public eye, we still follow these unspoken rules in our interpersonal relationships. It's important to take notice and understand why, for example, calling a plus-sized girl brave for wearing a bikini to the beach isn't really a compliment. The bottom line: wear what makes you feel good about yourself and don't let any rules about what's flattering or unflattering, or acceptable or shocking dictate those decisions.

Health Concerns or Something Else?

Just as making comments about clothing being unflattering isn't about the clothes, the same applies to certain displays of concern for the health of others. A common misconception is that a person's fitness and health correspond directly to his or her weight. In reality, people of all shapes and sizes can be healthy—or unhealthy for that matter. A person of size can run a marathon. A skinny person can get winded after a handful of jumping jacks. Just because you can see the outside of a person does not mean you know anything about what's on the inside—literally—not just in a touchy-feely way (though that may also be true).

This is a common issue that many people may not even realize can be discriminatory or hurtful. Before you show concern about someone's health, which is in and of itself a personal subject, ask yourself what is at the root of your concern. Is it because you have noticed changes or problems with the way this person is acting? It's one thing to show concern for a friend who has suddenly become pale or just had a coughing fit. And it's another thing entirely to ask about a friend's health because he or she is skinnier or fatter than you consider normal.

Decide to pass on the cake? Say "no thanks," but there's no need to add a moral judgment such as whether you should or can afford to eat it.

In a similar vein, comments about what you should or should not eat can be a code or shorthand for what you are expected to look like. If someone offers you a slice of cake at a birthday party, you might say something such as, "Oh, no thanks. I shouldn't." In most instances the "shouldn't" isn't because of a health condition like diabetes. It's because you are trying to maintain a certain weight or even lose a little. The phrase, "I'm watching what I eat," is code for "watching my weight." People of size get surprising comments and judgments from others based on what they eat. That's easy to avoid doing. But make an effort not to say those things about yourself either. The people around you will take your words as cues that apply to them as well.

On the other side of this coin, there's a bit of body shaming that lurks underneath a compliment or congratulations for someone who has lost weight. Though it may seem like a positive thing to tell people that you're impressed or that they look great now that they have lost those fifteen pounds, what that statement reinforces is something negative. Again and again our society rewards those who fit into a narrow definition of what attractive is. To praise people who previously fell outside of that definition and now have conformed is to tell them that this is the only way to be attractive.

"Did you lose weight?"

"Yes, I lost ten pounds."

"Wow, it really shows!"

Medical Fat Shaming: A Potentially Fatal Bias

Even medical professionals can make quick judgments based on a person's weight, which can lead to misdiagnoses. This unfortunately happens often enough that there's a term for it: medical fat shaming. In 2014, a woman named Catherine Carelli slipped on ice and broke her leg in several places, including her knee. When she consulted a surgeon, he refused to treat her because she was "so fat." He told her to let the leg heal and lose weight before he would replace her knee. Luckily, Carelli got a second opinion from another surgeon who operated on her the next week, fixing her leg.

An even more extreme example is Rebecca Hiles, who at age nineteen started to experience breathlessness. She was a dancer, and she now had trouble walking. When she started coughing up blood, she visited the emergency room, where she was told that if she lost weight, her immune system would be stronger. Her symptoms got more and more serious, causing her to vomit often and

(continued on the next page)

(continued from the previous page)

sleep sitting up so she could breathe. Five whole years later, a pulmonologist thought to order a CT scan. It turned out that she had lung cancer, and the lower half of one of her lungs had turned black from decay. Luckily, she survived, but if it had been caught earlier, she would have kept her lung. Even doctors sometimes make the mistake of not looking beyond the weight or BMI (body mass index) of the patient. Though our actions usually have fewer life-and-death repercussions, there is still a lesson to be learned from these cases.

It feels good to get compliments on your appearance, especially if you have worked hard to diet and exercise to achieve a certain goal. The goal need not be based on your weight, though, but on your mental and physical health and well-being. Getting compliments on your appearance after a recent weight loss sends the message that your "before" body wasn't good enough.

Another reason to avoid praising someone based on a change in weight is that it could have been caused by something other than diet and exercise. There's always a chance that a weight change could be the result of a medical condition or recent illness. Circling back to health, this just reinforces the notion that you aren't able to divine someone's health based on appearance. Not everyone who loses or gains weight has done it by choice.

Stopping the Cycle

There may not be a way to completely prevent all negative conversations around our appearances. We know they come up, so the only way to stop the cycle of body negativity is to learn ways to end or change the conversation. Start with yourself: try to stop from making negative comments about your own body, even in a joking way. If you compliment someone, don't denigrate yourself in the process. You can tell someone that he or she looks good and leave it at that. Putting yourself down doesn't make the compliment mean more. So, there's no need to compare or measure the appearances of others with yourself.

If someone gives you a backhanded compliment that it looks like you've lost weight or makes a playful remark about the second cookie you ate after dinner, you don't have to respond at all. You can look at the person, acknowledging that you heard what was said, and not say anything back to show that you don't

Help your friends see something positive when they look in the mirror instead of whatever they see as their flaws.

appreciate it. Or, you can ask a simple question to reflect it back to him or her: "Why do you ask?"

Pay attention to how you respond when people body shame themselves. If a friend says, "I feel so fat," try not to respond by assuring her that she's not fat. You can instead affirm that she looks great instead of setting those two concepts as opposites. If your friend complains about a part of her body, resist jumping in with a negative comment about your own to boost her up. Likely, this will just result in the battle of who looks worse, and you'll both lose. Instead, you can point out something positive about your friend's body. Even if she isn't feeling confident about how her body looks, she can still celebrate the things it can do, whether that means strength, flexibility, or the best moves on the dance floor.

CHAPTER FIVE

Taking Positive Action

I t's important to learn how to take care of yourself to keep feeling positively about your body. That means taking care of both your mental and your physical health. You can exercise your mind to train it out of negative habits just like you would exercise your body to train for a race. What you see when you look in the mirror shouldn't only be how many push-ups you did this week but what kinds of stories you are telling yourself about your body, too.

Self-Care for the Win

We get messages from many different directions every day telling us what defines an attractive, acceptable, or normal body. The messages come from all sides: magazines, ads, images on our social media feeds, and the list goes on. Though you can't eliminate all the negative input, you can make conscious decisions to limit some of the influences that you notice having a detrimental

Actor Jennifer Lawrence poses for a photo shoot at the Cannes Film Festival. Many glamour shots like this one fill the pages of magazines and can perpetuate unrealistic beauty standards.

effect on your own body image. In order to do that, check in with yourself: if that fitness magazine you subscribe to makes you feel more guilty than inspired, cancel your subscription; if you find yourself comparing your thighs to Jennifer Lawrence's instead of enjoying the celebrity gossip, put down that issue of *People*. You may notice that your friends pick apart the appearances, eating habits, or fitness routines of those around them. Question whether those people care about you as a whole person or if the surface is what they're more interested in.

When you're on social media, what does your feed look like? If it's a sea of diet trends, airbrushed selfies, and fitspiration images, ask yourself if looking at all of that makes you happy. The great thing about any type of social media is that it's personalized. You are the one who chooses which people and organizations to follow. If you come away from perusing your Instagram feed feeling worse about yourself than you did before you checked it, switch it up. Find things that make you happy, whether it's silly animal videos or inspirational quotes, and add some of that to the mix. You can make the conscious effort to surround yourself with as many positive messages, influences, and people as you can. Anything (or anyone) that makes you feel your body isn't good enough can be removed with one easy click. Not everything is that simple, so why not make it easy on yourself when you can?

Social (Media) Anxiety

Here are some ways social media influences body consciousness.

- Platforms like Facebook, Instagram, and Snapchat are largely visual, which allows teens to seek and earn approval for their appearance as well as compare themselves to others. (Which photo got the most likes?)

- Filters and free apps allow anyone to alter his or her appearance with ease. You don't need advanced Photoshop skills to make your waist smaller or your skin poreless and pimple-free. The control this gives you is deceptive. Does doctoring a selfie before you post it make you feel better about your body when you walk out the door in the morning?

- The fitness and wellness industry has boomed across social media. A 2016 analysis showed that fifty fitspiration websites used language and images that were sometimes interchangeable with those of pro-anorexia (pro-ana or thinspiration) sites. Both used guilt-inducing language about weight, stigmatized fat/weight, encouraged restraint/dieting, and used objectifying phrases.

(continued on the next page)

73

(continued from the previous page)

- Think of how much time you spend on social media each day. That means during that time, you are constantly bombarded with images of celebrities' toned abs and arms and ads and promotional posts on dieting and fitness trends, not to mention all the images your friends post of themselves. Scrolling through Instagram or Facebook, you may not be examining all these images with the same critical eye you would magazine covers or movie imagery.

Staying Body Positive Amid All the Negativity

Whether you're in a dining hall, locker room, or fitting room, it's hard not to fall into the habit of using negative or judgmental language about the body, especially when you're surrounded by it. But staying body positive will not only keep you feeling good about yourself, it will also help stop the cycle of body shaming among others around you. There are a few key ways you can do this, but at the root of them all is awareness. If you make a conscious effort to recognize body shaming when it occurs around you or on social media and even those

No one likes to be the subject of negative gossip. There's no need to criticize anyone else's body, whether or not they're within earshot.

negative thoughts you have yourself, you can take steps to make sure you don't perpetuate it.

Gossiping is a fact of our culture and our social lives, but that doesn't mean it's acceptable to make comments about other people's bodies, in front of them or behind their backs. If your friends start engaging in this kind of talk, you don't have to participate. Rather, you can say something nice about whomever they are discussing. You can even choose to be direct about the fact that you don't enjoy criticizing people because of their bodies. If you aren't comfortable with either of these options, you can stay quiet and just opt out of the conversation entirely. If this type of talk comes up often, these friends may not be the positive influences you want in your inner circle.

Seek out the people who are there for you, who make you feel good about yourself. Those are the friends you want to keep around. You can create your own social circle of body-positive people, and it will become that much easier to feel comfortable and confident in your own skin. If your friend says something that makes you feel bad about your body, it's also possible he doesn't know the effect his words have. If you explain, he may end up changing his tune. Take note of toxic people and influences and see if you can remove them from your life. If it makes you feel bad about your body, you don't need it in your life.

Note to Self: You're Awesome!

Remind yourself every day that there are positive things about your body and things about your body you are thankful for. Telling yourself one or two of those things daily can have a powerful effect on your self-image. They can be simple statements, such as, "I am beautiful," "My weight doesn't define who I am," or "I love my body just the way it is today." These may seem cheesy or obvious, but they actually work. You're not just saying them until you believe them. You are also taking time each day to take note of your own thoughts about yourself. They can help you notice the unconscious negative thoughts about yourself that you have throughout the day and begin to learn to quiet them. A very easy way to do this is to leave yourself notes on your mirror. Every time you look into it, you won't just see your reflection. You'll also see a reminder of something great about it. Eventually, you may look in the mirror and focus on what you love rather than what you'd like to change.

Reframe That Picture

No body is perfect, but rather than focus on imperfections and flaws, concentrate on the things that

Rather than feeling self-conscious about a scar, try to wear it with pride—as evidence of a challenge that you've overcome and put behind you.

make you unique and all the great things that your body can do. Everyone has something about their body that they don't like or that they feel particularly insecure about, but it doesn't have to be the main thing you zoom in on every time you look in the mirror. Instead, come up with positive things about your body and focus on those. There will always be things and people in your environment that send negative messages about body image; however, what you tell yourself about your own body is something you can work to improve. Remind yourself that looks aren't everything. Though it's a clichéd phrase, there is also truth to it. There are so many things your body can do and has done. Rather than looking at scars as blemishes, see them as evidence of a challenge you have overcome, testimony of your body's ability to heal itself. Whenever possible, try to take something that you see as a flaw and reframe it into something positive.

Also take note of all the things beyond how your body looks that make you proud to be yourself. Maybe you're a great dancer or you love playing soccer. Appreciate the ways your body can move, your strength, and the things your body does that you may even be proud of.

You can also reframe your goals to reflect how you want to *feel* rather than how you want to look.

Spread Kindness, Crush Stereotypes

Come up with ways to spread kindness and put more goodness out there. In response to teens being bullied online, students have created Twitter accounts devoted to tweeting personalized compliments to their classmates instead. A high school in Vermont started a Positive Post-It campaign after a scourge of hateful messages started appearing in an app called After School. They petitioned Apple to have the product removed from the Apple Store, and their Positive Post-It campaign had students posting affirming and supportive notes on walls throughout the school. The idea was simple, but the result was moving. To walk down a hallway and see all the kind things people have to say about one another rather than nasty insults can be empowering for everyone.

Don't be afraid to crush stereotypes. Just because your body does not conform to a certain standard it does not mean you cannot do what you love. Akira Armstrong is a professional dancer who was having trouble finding an agent to represent her because—despite performing as a backup dance in two Beyoncé videos—her body did not conform to the standards that dancers' bodies are expected to. She started her own dance company, called Pretty Big Movement, that features full-figured dancers like herself who can dance just as well as any of the long and lean dancers our society is used to seeing. Together, they opened a dance studio where women of all body types can show off their moves and have a great time doing it without fear of any judgment.

Many exercise and diet regimes are centered around the goal of a number on a scale or tape measure. These aren't the types of goals that foster a positive feeling about your body. Change the way you set your goals so that you are focusing on your health—both mental and physical. For example, instead of going running to try to lose weight, start training for a race. Maybe you will discover you really love running if you focus on how far you can go or beating your best time around the track instead of how much weight you've lost.

Finding a physical activity you actually enjoy will help you practice body positivity. It'll boost your endorphins, bust some stress, and in turn, improve

Rather than focusing on a number on a scale, it can be much more satisfying to train for an event or race against yourself to beat your personal record.

your own self image. The most important thing is to find what works for you and what makes you feel the best. If you like to do yoga or Pilates YouTube videos at home to let go of the stress of the day, go for it. If you're the type of person who prefers to be more social about physical activity, find a friend who likes to do the same activities as you or maybe join a team.

CHAPTER SIX

Moving Beyond Shaming

It is helpful to know the reasons that cause people to body shame others and the factors that cause us to feel shame about our own bodies. There are strategies to limit the amount of body-negative messages we see each day and strategies to try to get the people around us to stop talking critically about the bodies of others. There are physical activities and mental exercises that can reduce your negative thoughts about your body and improve your self-image. There may also be times when body shaming goes too far and you may not know how to stop it. Though it's helpful to learn different ways to deal with body shaming, it is also important to know when the issue is too serious to deal with on your own.

Acknowledge What Is Happening

When you notice body shaming happen—whether it happens to someone in your social group, on

Instead of focusing on your looks, make time for activities that make you happy. Honing a skill like music or drawing can give you pride that's more than skin deep.

social media, or to you—it is important to be honest about what is happening. If you feel comfortable doing so, confront the person who has done the body shaming. You don't have to be combative to make it clear what he or she said is not OK. Whether the body shaming is happening to you or someone else, you can say that those words have made you uncomfortable. It doesn't matter who the shamer is talking about because whether the person criticized your looks or someone else's, it's still inappropriate to make those comments. There's a strong chance those comments have made more people uncomfortable than just the person being shamed.

Whether you are able to speak up or not, it is important to examine the effect that body shaming has on you. Even if you don't tell the bully how it made you feel, you still need to acknowledge those feelings for yourself. Has it made you more self-conscious? Has it changed your behavior at all? Think about the way you interact with people and the activities you do. Has anything shifted in the aftermath of body shaming (even if you were just a witness)? The difference might be subtle, such as deciding not to post that picture of you at the beach on social media. Maybe you even decided to keep your T-shirt or coverup on at the beach that day when you didn't used to do that. Body shaming might have even changed what you choose to eat now. It is important to listen to your inner voice

The choices you make daily—both big and small—should be based on your health and happiness rather than guilt or shame over how you look.

and understand how your feelings about yourself have been affected.

Just as your behavior may start to shift in the wake of body shaming, it could happen to a friend or family member just as easily. Just as you can become more observant about when and how body shaming happens, you can also begin recognizing signs when someone in your life is suffering from body shaming's hurtful effects.

Talk Is Priceless

Body shaming should not be dealt with alone. You shouldn't ever feel like you have to keep your feelings to yourself and get past them on your own. Go to someone you trust and can confide in. It is likely that this person will do more than just sympathize. He or she likely has a similar experience to share. It will make you feel better to know you are not alone. Whomever you have chosen to confide in will be

Talk to someone who cares about you instead of keeping your negative feelings to yourself. They can remind you what they love about you or share similar experiences they've had.

someone who cares about you. This person will be able to share many positive things about you that he or she appreciates. You can repeat affirmations in the mirror, and that does help improve self-image, but in the wake of something hurtful, it will help you to have someone else around who can remind you of reasons why you're great. Maybe this person's perspective is different than yours.

The person you turn to when you are dealing with body shaming will be someone close to you whom you trust and will appreciate things about you that you either did not notice or took for granted. They may be about your appearance, like how much this person loves your smile or dimples. But your trusted confidant will probably have reasons deeper than that for why you should feel good about yourself. Maybe you're loyal, good at making people laugh when they've had a bad day, or always able to find the perfect gift. It will be helpful to be reminded of those things. How can you assure yourself of them if you don't even notice them? That's why it's so important to have someone you can turn to.

A friend or family member can stand up for you, comfort you if you're upset, and come up with suggestions and strategies to make you feel better. It is always better to deal with a problem with help. Someone who cares about you will make you feel valued and might take some of the weight and importance away from negative things others may have said about your body.

Getting Help When You Need It

You may have a good idea of what body shaming is and the many forms it can take, but it can still be hard to tell when you can handle the situation and when it is serious enough that you won't be able to deal with the effects alone. Body shame is very personal, and it may feel embarrassing or even humiliating to go to an adult you may not know very well for help—even with the knowledge that the adult is a trained professional such as a therapist or guidance counselor. You may not know whom to ask in order to find a professional who can help.

If your concern is over a friend, you may be afraid that involving someone else would violate his or her privacy. What if your friend gets mad at you for telling someone else the thoughts and feelings he or she shared with you in confidence? In situations like this, ask yourself a few questions to help assess the severity of the situation.

- Has someone been body shaming your friend on a regular basis?
- Have you noticed changes in your friend's behavior, such as becoming less social, more

Sometimes the support of friends and family isn't enough to help someone suffering from body shame. It's important to recognize when that person may need outside help.

easily embarrassed, or nervous?

* Have you noticed any changes in his or her eating or exercise habits?

These are merely general questions to help you notice if body shaming has either gotten out of control or had a serious effect on someone you care about.

Though it is a hard choice, it may be more important that this person get the help needed, even if it means he or she gets upset with you for telling someone. Later on when she or he has more perspective or gets over the initial embarrassment, he or she will hopefully come to understand that you were acting out of concern and care for him or her. If you believe that body shame is changing the way your friend lives his or her life, it is time to get someone involved who is better equipped to handle the problem.

If you are the one being body shamed, and you don't know how to make it stop, it may be time for you to seek outside help for your own well-being. Ask yourself similar questions to the ones you would ask if it were happening to a friend: have you internalized criticisms of your body and started to think negative thoughts about your body as a result? Have you changed any of your behavior because of body shame? This could be anything from eating habits, to the way you dress, to what activities you feel comfortable participating in. Do you feel more anxious or depressed?

Body shame is not something anyone should deal with on their own. When negative feelings about your body interfere with your daily life, cause an increase in anxiety or depression, or develop into behavior associated with eating disorders, it is time to find a professional to help. Tell a trusted adult, such as a family member, teacher, or guidance counselor, how you have been feeling. This person will either be able to help you or guide you to a trained professional such as a therapist who can work through it with you.

10 Great Questions to Ask a Counselor

1. How do I deal with the feelings I have from being body shamed?

2. I think someone may have body shamed me, but I'm not sure. How can I tell if I have been body shamed?

3. Members of my family tend to make comments on my body that make me feel like it isn't good enough the way it is. What should I do?

4. I have been having negative thoughts about my body or have found myself comparing it with the bodies of other people. How can I control or prevent these thoughts?

5. Someone I know has been body shamed. How can I help him or her?

6. How can I exercise so that it will be enjoyable, instead of focused on changing how I look?

7. How can I work on getting others to understand that people are not all supposed to be the same size, shape, and build?

(continued on the next page)

10 Great Questions to Ask a Counselor

(continued from the previous page)

8. How can I work on accepting my body for the way it is today?

9. What can I do to improve my self-worth and value other aspects about myself besides my appearance?

10. How can I learn to change the conversation with my friends so that it isn't focused on body flaws or exercise and food guilt?

Glossary

affirmation A short, positive statement that you make to yourself in an effort to change a negative subconscious thought process. It helps draw attention to your subconscious thoughts and shift your thinking in a positive direction.

airbrushing Refers to any retouching of a photo that changes the appearance of the person in it, from erasing acne or pores on the skin to changing the shape of the body or face.

anorexia Also known as anorexia nervosa, this is an eating disorder in which people develop an extreme fixation about their weight and what they eat.

BMI Stands for body mass index. It is a formula that uses height and weight to estimate body fat.

CT scan Stands for computerized tomography scan. By combining several Xray images taken at different angles, it shows cross-sections of the bones, soft tissues, and blood vessels. It gives you more information than Xrays alone.

denigrate Criticize or put down unfairly.

detrimental Tending to cause harm or damage.

discriminatory Describes the unfair treatment of a person or group based on prejudice toward that person or group.

emaciated Abnormally thin to the point of it being a health concern, especially caused by illness or lack of food.

exclusionary   When an act or policy is characterized by leaving out a group or groups.

internalize   To absorb an opinion, idea, or belief so that it becomes part of how you see yourself.

medical fat shaming   A phenomenon where a medical practitioner makes choices or even errors based on weight bias rather than the patient as a whole.

microaggression   A statement or action that either subtly or unintentionally discriminates against or shows hostility toward members of a marginalized group.

normalization   The processes by which something comes to be seen as normal or natural in daily life.

Photoshop   To digitally alter an image using the photo-editing software Photoshop.

postpartum   The period of time after childbirth.

pulmonologist   Doctor who specializes in the treatment and diagnosis of lung conditions and diseases.

self-deprecation   Belittling or criticizing yourself, sometimes in a way that is meant to be humorous.

trigger   Something that sets off a memory or reminder of a negative experience, which can cause an emotional response.

validate To demonstrate or support the truth or value of something—a belief, feeling, statement, and so forth.

volatile Threatening to change unpredictably and quickly, usually in a negative direction.

For More Information

About-Face

PO Box 191145

San Francisco, CA 94119

(415) 839-6779

Website: http://www.about-face.org

Facebook: @aboutfacesf

Twitter: @aboutfacesf

This organization's mission is to help women and girls understand and resist harmful messages from the media that negatively affect their body image. It does so through activism, education, and outreach.

The Alliance for Eating Disorders Awareness

1649 Forum Place #2

West Palm Beach, FL 33401

(866) 662-1235

Website: http://www.allianceforeatingdisorders .com

A nonprofit organization providing outreach, education, and early intervention programs for all eating disorders.

Media Awareness Network

205 Catharine Street, Suite 100

Ottawa, ON K2P 1C3

Canada

(613) 224-7721

Website: http://mediasmarts.ca/digital-media
-literacy/media-issues/body-image

The Media Awareness Network strives to educate
Canadian children and teens about the way the
media affects body image. It also provides lesson
plans and worksheets for parents to help them
talk to their kids about these issues.

National Association to Advance Fat Acceptance
(NAAFA)

PO Box 4662

Foster City, CA 94404-0662

(916) 558-6880

Website: http://www.naafaonline.com

This nonprofit civil rights organization aims to end
size discrimination through advocacy, public
education, and support.

National Eating Disorder Information Centre (NEDIC)

ES 7-421, 200 Elizabeth Street

Toronto, ON M5G 2C4

Canada

(866) 633-4220

Website: http://nedic.ca

The National Eating Disorder Information Centre focuses on the awareness and prevention of food and weight preoccupation and eating disorders through a variety of educational outreach including workshops, presentations, and webinars. It also has a toll-free helpline that provides support and/or treatment options for people across Canada affected by these issues.

National Eating Disorders Association (NEDA)

165 West 46th Street, Suite 402

New York, NY 10036

(800) 931-2237

Website: http://nationaleatingdisorders.org

Facebook: @NationalEatingDisordersAssociation

Twitter: @NEDAstaff

Instagram: @NEDA

NEDA offers programs and services to support

individuals and families affected by eating disorders. It has a hotline and also provides educational materials online about prevention and detection, and how to get help.

Websites

Because of the changing nature of internet links, Rosen Publishing has developed an online list of websites related to the subject of this book. This site is updated regularly. Please use this link to access this list:

http://www.rosenlinks.com/COP/Body

For Further Reading

Czerniawski, Amanda M. *Fashioning Fat: Inside Plus-Size Modeling.* New York, NY: New York University Press, 2015.

Green, Megan. *Body Image and Body Shaming.* New York, NY: Lucent Press, 2017.

Klein, Melanie, and Anna Guest-Jelley. *Yoga and Body Image: 25 Personal Stories About Beauty, Bravery & Loving Your Body.* Woodbury, MN: Llwellyn Publications, 2014.

Leviathan, David. *Hold Me Closer: The Tiny Cooper Story.* New York, NY: Dutton Books, 2015.

Mackler, Carolyn. *The Earth, My Butt, and Other Big Round Things.* Cambridge, MA: Candlewick Press, 2003.

Murphy, Julie. *Dumplin'.* New York, NY: HarperCollins Publishers, 2015.

Niven, Jennifer. *Holding Up the Universe.* New York, NY: Alfred A. Knopf, 2016.

O'Neill, Louise. *Only Ever Yours.* London, United Kingdom: Quercus Books, 2015.

Orr, Tamra. *Combatting Body Shaming.* New York, NY: Rosen Publishing Group, 2017.

Sayre, Justin. *Husky.* New York: NY: Penguin Young Readers Group, 2015.

Stanley, Jessamyn. *Every Body Yoga: Let Go of Fear, Get On the Mat, Love Your Body.* New York, NY: Workman Publishing, 2017.

Weiss, Dara Lynn. *The Heavy: A Mother, a Daughter, a Diet*. New York, NY: Ballantine Books, 2013.

Wilcox, Christine. *Teens and Body Image*. San Diego, CA: Referencepoint Press, 2015.

Youngs, Jennifer Leigh. *Health & Fitness for Teens*. Burres Books, 2014.

Bibliography

Adams, Rebecca, "It's Not Just Girls. Boys Struggle With Body Image, Too." *Huffington Post*, December 29, 2014. http://www.huffingtonpost.com/2014/09/17/body-image-boys_n_5637975.html.

Baker, Jes. *Things No One Will Tell Fat Girls: A Handbook of Unapologetic Living.* Berkeley, CA: Seal Press, 2015.

Beauty Redefined. "Photoshopping: Altering Images and Our Minds." *Beauty Redefined*, March 12, 2014. http://www.beautyredefined.net/photoshopping-altering-images-and-our-minds.

Brown, Harriet. *Body of Truth: How Science, History, and Culture Drive Our Obsession with Weight—And What We Can Do About It.* Boston, MA: Da Capo Press, 2015.

Brown, Harriet. "These Women Were Fat-Shamed by Their Doctors—And It Almost Cost Them Their Lives." *Prevention Magazine,* October 29, 2015. http://www.prevention.com/health/medical-fat-shaming.

Burton, Natasha. "Long, Necks, Stretched Lips, and Other Beauty Standards from Around the World." *Cosmopolitan*, June 6, 2013. http://www.cosmopolitan.com/style-beauty/g3279/weird-beauty.

Coen, Jessica, "Here Are the Unretouched Images from Lena Dunham's *Vogue* Shoot." *Jezebel*, January 17, 2014. http://jezebel.com/here-are-the-unretouched-images-from-lena-dunhams-vogu-1503336657.

Czerniawski, Amanda M. *Fashioning Fat: Inside Plus-Size Modelling*. New York, NY: New York University Press, 2015.

Eisenberg, Marla E., Melanie Wall, and Diane Neumark-Sztainer. "Muscle-Enhancing Behaviors Among Adolescent Girls and Boys." *Pediatrics* 130 (December 2012) 6: 1019–1026.

France, Lisa Respers, "Lady Gaga Responds to Super Bowl Body Shaming." *CNN*, February 8, 2017. http://www.cnn.com/2017/02/08/entertainment/lady-gaga-body-shamed.

Frank, Priscilla, "Pretty Big Movement Is a Dance Company That Crushes Body Stereotypes With Style." *Huffington Post*, January 13, 2017. http://www.huffingtonpost.com/entry/body-positive-dance-company_us_5877979ce4b03c8a02d59e6f.

HelloMagazine.com. "Kate Winslet's New Contract Bans Retouching of Her Photos." *Hello*, October 23, 2015. http://us.hellomagazine.com/healthandbeauty/skincare-and-fragrances/2015102327855/kate-winslet-will-no-longer-let-adverts-be-retouched/.

Klein, Melanie, and Anna Guest-Jelley. *Yoga and Body Image: 25 Personal Stories About Beauty, Bravery & Loving Your Body.* Woodbury, MN: Llewellyn Publications, 2014.

Klein, Sarah. "How to Get Into Yoga at Any Size." *Prevention Magazine*, June 10, 2016. http://www.huffingtonpost.com/2013/05/29/yoga-for-selfacceptance-5_n_3348153.html.

"Lena Dunham Happy Cellulite not Airbrushed for Glamour Cover." *BBC News*. January 5, 2017. http://www.bbc.com/news/entertainment-arts-38521025.

Patrick, Wendy L. *Red Flags: How to Spot Frenemies, Underminers, and Toxic People in Your Life.* New York, NY: St. Martin's Press, 2015.

"Revealed: How the 'Ideal' Male Body Changes Around the World." *Telegraph*. February 18, 2016. http://www.telegraph.co.uk/men/the-filter/revealed-how-the-ideal-male-body-changes-around-the-world.

Simmons, Rachel. "How Social Media Is a Toxic Mirror." *Time.com*, August 19, 2016. http://time.com/4459153/social-media-body-image/.

Stoeffel, Kat. "Sad, 'Fat-Shaming' Lululemon Founder Steps Down." *New York*, December 10, 2013. http://nymag.com/thecut/2013/12/sad-lululemon-founder-steps-down.html.

Whitefield-Madrano, Autumn. *Face Value: The Hidden Ways Beauty Shapes Women's Lives.* New York, NY: Simon & Schuster, 2016.

Willets, Melissa. "Kids Start to Feel Body Shame Younger Than Ever, Survey Says." *Parenting*, May 18, 2017. http://www.parenting.com/news -break/kids-start-to-feel-body-shame-younger -ever-survey-says.

Woolf, Emma. *The Ministry of Thin: How the Pursuit of Perfection Got Out of Control.* Berkeley, CA: Soft Skull Press, 2014.

Index

About the Author

Natalie Chomet is an author and marketer of children's and young adult educational resources. She graduated from Vassar College with a BA in English and a strong background in gender studies. From age six, she has studied dance, ballet and Martha Graham modern, in particular. Fortunate enough to learn from teachers and institutions who were body positive and inclusive, Chomet has experienced the positive effects dance can have on self-image. She enjoys reading, doing yoga, and learning the lindy hop in her spare time. Chomet currently resides in Brooklyn, New York.

Photo Credits

Cover SpeedKingz/Shutterstock.com; p. 5 Ronald Martinez/Getty Images; p. 9 Biris Paul Silviu/Moment Mobile/Getty Images; p. 13 danekalbo/iStock/Thinkstock; pp. 14–15 luanateutzi/Shutterstock.com; p. 19 Michael Ochs Archives/Moviepix/Getty Images; p. 23 Highwaystarz-Photography/iStock/Thinkstock; pp. 26–27 Richard Sharrocks/Alamy Stock Photo; pp. 30, 69 Featureflash Photo Agency/Shutterstock.com; pp. 34–35 Rob Stark/Shutterstock.com; p. 39 s_bukley/Shutterstock.com; pp. 40–41 AntonioGuillem/iStock/Thinkstock; pp. 46–47 Bloomberg/Getty Images; p. 49 diego_cervo/iStock/Thinkstock; p. 51 nito100/iStock/Thinkstock; pp. 52–53 fizkes/Shutterstock.com; pp. 56–57 Joe Raedle/Getty Images; p. 58 Jupiterimages/Creatas/Thinkstock; pp. 60-61 fizkes/iStock/Thinkstock; pp. 66–67 monkeybusinessimages/iStock/Thinkstock; p.73©iStockphoto.com/Highwaystarz-Photography;p.76ajr_images/iStock/Thinkstock; pp. 80–81 CreativaImages/iStock/Thinkstock; p. 83 Photodisc/Thinkstock; p. 85 BananaStock/Thinkstock; pp. 86–87 DragonImages/iStock/Thinkstock; p. 90 Wavebreakmedia Ltd/Thinkstock; cover and interior pages background © iStockphoto.com/Sergei Dubrovski.

Design and Layout: Nicole Russo-Duca; Editor and Photo Research: Heather Moore Niver